THE EAST KENT LIGH[T]

Mat[t]

"A history of the line in combination with the Kent coal field"

Above: East Kent Railway locomotive No. 7 at Sandwich Road with one of the short-lived Richborough line passenger services, 22 September 1928. *(Lens of Sutton)*

Published by
Matthew Beddall
26 St. Martin's Hill
Canterbury
CT1 1PP
Copyright © 1998

ISBN 0 9532952 0 6

INTRODUCTION

The East Kent Light Railway has a very colourful history, being typical of Colonel Stephens' idyllic rural light railways. The Colonel's economies gave rise to the railway's character, with its wooden buildings, tatty engines and infrequent services, all of which created an ambience unique to the line. The line was often referred to as Stephens' "biggest disappointment". Whether he ever uttered those words is unknown, but there is evidence of some truth in the statement. The modern day East Kent Railway is quite different, but still evokes some of the primitive charm of the light railway atmosphere. This chronicle illustrates the line from its conception, through to its rebirth as a passenger carrying light railway, in combination with the Kent coal field.

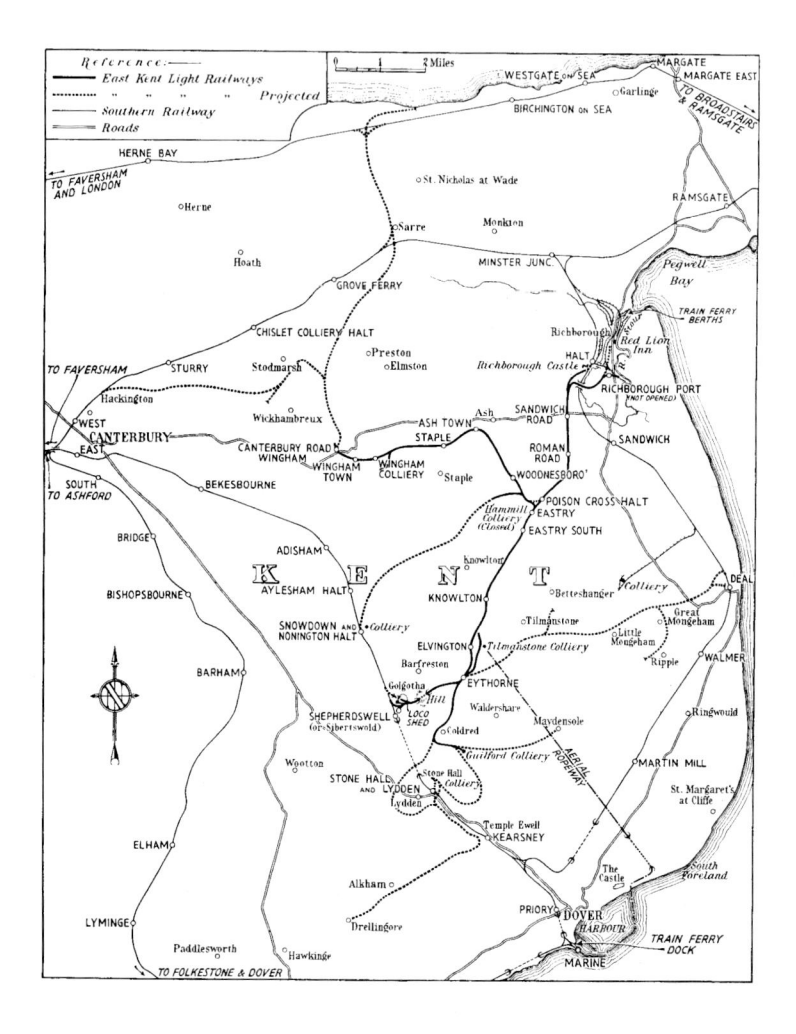

Above: A map of the East Kent Light Railway, courtesy *The Railway Magazine*

THE STORY BEGINS...

At the end of the 19th Century while pilot borings were sunk at Shakespeare Cliff (Dover) for a Channel Tunnel large coal deposits were found. The discovery confirmed the predictions of nineteenth-century geologists, who foretold that East Kent would have rich coal seams below. Kent's coal industry was destined to grow from this almost accidental beginning, together with the aspirations of its pioneers. These high aspirations were inevitably doomed to be disappointed, with the consequent developments being a mere shadow of what was originally expected.

The Channel Tunnel project was side-lined as digging began for Dover Colliery, at Shakespeare Cliff. Despite work on the Channel Tunnel being put into abeyance, the plans were not finally abandoned until 1930. The discovery of coal led to over 40 other shafts being sunk throughout East Kent, all within a short space of time. Dover Colliery proved to be a very limited success, having to close due to flooding. Despite a very short life it served as the start of the Kent coal field story.

No time was wasted as pits were hastily developed across East Kent, most noticeably Wingham, Tilmanstone, Guilford, Snowdown, Stone Hall, Shakespeare Cliff and Woodnesborough. The best coal was found some 1500 feet down, with digging eventually extending far under the seabed. The workforce for this rapidly expanding industry was mostly provided from the Midlands, the North (especially Yorkshire) and from Wales. It was later to emerge that the newcomers would bring with them the militant attitudes of elsewhere in the British coal industry.

The combination of primitive transport and a need to move large volumes of equipment resulted in a group of colliery owners conceiving the need for a railway. Under the original application in 1910 the new line was promoted as the East Kent Minerals Light Railway. It quickly became known as the East Kent Light Railway when at the first Public Enquiry local representatives suggested that it should not just be used for mineral traffic. The line was to take advantage of the Light Railways Act of 1896, allowing it to be built at a considerable economy.

The East Kent Light Railways Company was promoted by the Kent Coal Concessions, in conjunction with other allied groups. One of the Kent coal field's most intriguing characters was Mr Arthur Burr. Together with his son and mining engineer, Dr Malcom Burr, he became involved in a confusing entanglement of companies. Whilst Arthur Burr helped provide momentum to the project, his financial dealings were, and still are, frowned upon.

All together about 40 different Light Railway Orders were applied for. The planned line ran from a junction with the South Eastern and Chatham Railway main line at Shepherdswell to Richborough Port, by way of Eastry. Tilmanstone Colliery would be served by a connection branching from Eythorne, which would rejoin the main line north of the Colliery. Another line would run to Guilford Colliery also from Eythorne. A route was planned to Canterbury through Wingham, which would diverge off at Eastry. After a Public Enquiry held at Canterbury on 17 and 18 October 1910 the plans had to be modified. Essentially this involved omitting the section beyond Wingham after objections from the War Office, Ecclesiastical Commissioners, and the South Eastern and Chatham Railway.

In November 1910, before approval of the initial application, the Company undertook a further order for an extra 10½ miles. The proposals were to serve other borings, as well as a line to Great Mongeham, near Deal. Subsequent to a Public Enquiry at Dover the application was approved.

On 19 June 1911 the Board of Trade granted a Light Railway Order. On the same date the East Kent Light Railways Company Limited was incorporated with an authorised share capital of £240,000. The contract for construction was awarded to the East Kent Contract and Financial Company Limited, one of the multitude of companies promoted by Arthur Burr. This involved Mr Holman Fred Stephens as the line's engineer, then subsequently as the General Manager and Locomotive Superintendent. Stephens had already proved himself as a light railway engineer. He had a reputation for economy and his influence was to become noticeable as the line developed. Stephens' empire of light railways had an atmosphere of their own, which was soon to extend into East Kent.

Above: A group of navvies at work on the construction of the line in the cutting approaching Eythorne. The girl in the picture is probably accompanying her father, and making the most of the opportunity to be photographed. *(Ken Elks Collection)*

Stephens estimated the cost under the original application would be £173,641. In December 1911 a temporary contractor's line was opened, between the main line at Shepherdswell and Tilmanstone Colliery. The temporary line ran around Golgotha Hill, although the exact route is unclear. Once the tunnel was bored the line was laid in a chalk cutting and under Golgotha. The tunnel is unusual, as it was brick lined to double track specifications, but with only one side fully excavated. The earth works from Shepherdswell to Tilmanstone were constructed to double track specifications, in common with the ambitions of the line's promoters.

The Kentish Gazette of 26 April 1913 describes the Contractor's temporary line, from a meeting with the line's Traffic Manager, Mr H. M. Springgay;

"The temporary line has, as far as possible, been laid alongside the permanent way, and much of it has been constructed with first-class materials. The object of this is when the cuttings, banks, and other works have been completed, the greatest portion of the temporary line will be simply "slewed" (moved over) onto the permanent track, and much money must thereby be saved."

This account of the temporary line contradicts other evidence, which suggests that the temporary line was laid to a "basic" standard. The temporary line carried supplies to Tilmanstone Colliery, and brought spoil back for earth works at Shepherdswell. The temporary affair would appear to have been replaced by the line through the newly built tunnel in the latter half of 1913. *The Kentish Gazette* received regular reports of progress making quite a good, but possibly over-confident, record of the line's development.

A number of other possible routes were considered, including lines to Adisham or Bekesbourne, Deal or Walmer and Martin Mill. Yet another application was submitted in November 1911, which involved an extension from Wingham to Stodmarsh, and from Great Mongeham to Ripple. The estimated cost of this third phase was £36,637, but later had risen to £38,741. This time a Public Enquiry was held in Sandwich during March 1912, the application being ratified on 18 November 1912. The next day marked a further landmark in the Kent coalfield story, as Snowdown Colliery produced the first load of Kent coal.

The planned Eythorne triangle line would have formed a triangular junction with the mainline and Guilford Colliery line, at Eythorne. There has been some contention as to if this line was ever actually built. The earth works were almost certainly completed as they appear on the 1937 revision Ordnance Survey map. There is no evidence to say that the triangle was ever installed. It is possible that the triangle was laid, but did not last very long, almost certainly only being built as a contractor's line.

The East Kent Railway Company produced a prospectus for their issue of 50,000 shares, which gave an account of the developments so far.

"The Contractor's temporary line connecting Tilmanstone Colliery with the South Eastern and Chatham' main line at Shepherdswell has been in operation for 5 months, during which time it has carried upwards of 10,000 tons of material to the Colliery, the revenue from which has shown ample return on the capital outlay, besides effecting considerable economy for the Colliery in haulage charges and extraordinary traffic claims (for road damage by the Kent County Council)."

This chronicle of the early stages of the railway gave potential investors a very favourable outlook on the Company's future. The Company's activities never produced any considerable returns, their generous predictions having been damaged by the succession of unforeseen problems that the collieries had to tackle.

The line continued on from Eythorne, reaching Eastry by October 1912, at the same time as the line to Guilford Colliery. The line extended to Wingham Colliery, with a branch to Hammill Colliery later in the same year. Eastry was to become the junction for the branches to Wingham and Richborough. Beyond Eastry a bridge carried the line over Selson Lane, before the two lines diverged. The main line continued to Poison Cross, with the branch to Wingham sharply curving off to the left.

On 27 November 1912 locomotive No. 1 left its normal duties for the honour of hauling a train for the Company's investors, prior to the first Annual General Meeting. The train would have used the Contractor's line, as the permanent line under Golgotha was not yet ready. The Chairman gave the meeting optimistic reassurances over the future success of

Above: Kent and East Sussex Railway locomotive, *Northiam*, at work on the line. Information from a Wingham resident suggests that it was photographed in the cutting beyond Wingham Town station, towards Canterbury Road. *(Lens of Sutton)*

the project. Such was the mood that the Chairman even suggested that if they continued to have difficulties with the South Eastern and Chatham Railway, they should seek permission to construct a competing line to the outskirts of London. Further applications were deferred in May 1912 after receiving complaints. The outbreak of war delayed the subsequent application for a further 22 miles, which were eventually approved.

An application for further extensions was made in 1914, the surveyor being C. J. Elgar of Wingham. There was a scheme to construct a line to Birchington which was to connect up to a deep-water seaport, the promoters of which claimed that ships could load at all times of the year, as the jetty would be protected by natural sandbanks. This would have been much more functional than Richborough Port, which could only be used in favourable weather conditions.

On 4 February 1913 the shareholders in the Kent Coal Concessions group of Companies entertained Mr Arthur Burr to a banquet in Dover's Town Hall, where he was presented with the Honorary Freedom of the Ancient Cinque Port. Prior to the celebrations the Shareholders were given the opportunity to visit Tilmanstone Colliery, being transported over the temporary line from Shepherdswell. The *Kentish Gazette* from 8 February 1913 states that "between four and five hundred persons availed themselves of the opportunity". It is quite ironic that this number of people is a similar figure for the whole of 1947!

The Annual meeting in 1914 once more received a cheerful report from the Chairman, Arthur Burr, but the affairs of the Company at this stage were far from ideal. Tilmanstone Colliery had been in production since 12 March 1913, but progress at Wingham and Hammill had not been forthcoming. The borings at Stonehall had ceased by 1913. Work at Guilford Colliery was temporally abandoned due to substantial flooding in the autumn of 1914. Tilmanstone also suffered from flooding after a roof collapsed, which led to production stopping for a month in early 1914.

The section from Eythorne to Eastry became redundant to coal traffic in 1914, due to Wingham and Hammill Collieries closing, together with several other small collieries. The Hammill Colliery buildings were taken over by the Hammill Brick Company, which started production in 1928. The railway connection was retained for inward deliveries of coal, with the bricks being moved by the railway until road transport became more widespread.

Wingham Colliery also failed to become productive. Its failure was blamed on World War I, as there was a significant shortage of manpower. This is backed up by a story that all the mining engineers were German. The fact that the pilot borings did not continue beyond 50 feet is probably also connected with the shortage of finance that Kent's coal industry faced. The brick built buildings of the colliery are now part of Grain Harvesters, an animal feed stuffs factory and shop. Some of the rails for the original sidings are still visible in the floor of one of the buildings. A siding to the Wingham Engineering Works diverged off 400 yards west of Wingham Colliery Halt, and provided the railway with a source of further traffic. The firm was involved with agricultural steam engines, and regularly received materials by rail, together with deliveries of coal for their own steam engines.

Because work on the smaller collieries was halted by World War I, it is often suggested that the request to operate passenger services was a result of the declaration of war in August 1914, however the timing could have been coincidental. At this time the War Department decided to develop Richborough as a seaport, with a number of army bases being established there. Richborough became very active, a scene that was not to be repeated outside the hostilities of war.

Stephens played an active part in the war effort, serving with the Royal Engineers from 1914 to 1916 as Major Commanding, Kent (Fortress), posted to the Thames and Medway Defences. He retired from active service in 1916, gaining the rank of Lieutenant-Colonel. Hereafter he became simply known as the "Colonel" on his empire of railways.

A meeting was held between the Contract Company and it's allied companies not long after the declaration of war, at which it was agreed that all construction work on the line should be halted. Mr Arthur Burr and his son Dr Malcolm Burr resigned from the East Kent Railways Company and also their other Companies in 1914. They left the railway in a chaotic situation, with unfinished construction work. At this time the line was not officially open, and the goal of reaching Richborough had still not been met. The

Above: The first engine to run on the East Kent Railway at Ash, 18 April 1913. This 0-4-0T Barclay locomotive's stay was short-lived. This print is the only known record of its presence, although its existence corellates with a *Kentish Gazette* report. *(Ken Elks Collection.)*

Contractors still retained control of the line, despite construction having slowed. The Burr's financial interests in the Kent coalfield seem to have been well protected by their own actions. Despite the promises of untold fortunes the debenture and shareholders by contrast received little more than a free trip on the line!

It is thought that the delay in the line opening was a combination of a shortage of manpower during World War I, and the contractors being awkward. By October 1916 Mr Burr was being sued for alleged fraud, by both the South Eastern Coalfields Extensions Limited and the East Kent Contract and Finance Company. With the latter company holding the contract for the line's construction, this would suggest a good reason for the delays in the contractors handing the line over, probably having met financial difficulties. It would seem that Arthur Burr resigned at a convenient time to protect his own interests. Despite the Company's positive publicity it is known that they had difficulty paying the contractors for their work.

By the end of World War I the quantity of coal carried by the railway had shown a significant increase with 15,886 tons being transported in 1915, in comparison to 129,604 tons by 1918. Despite this growth the plans to develop East Kent as an industrial haven were soon lost as the rapid industrial expansion slowed.

The Light Railway Order of 1911 entitled the railway to operate passenger trains. The mainstay of the passenger traffic was expected to come from the rural areas, and the miners travelling to work. Miners' trains were shown on the time table as going directly to Tilmanstone Colliery, with special workmans tickets being available. The Company managed to take control of the line from their contractors in 1916. Eventually the works

Above: Tilmanstone Colliery, originally named East Kent Colliery. The photograph would have been taken in about 1910, and illustrates the impact that the colliery had on the landscape. *(Ken Elks Collection.)*

Above: A later view of Tilmanstone Colliery. Notice the Colliery's own wagons in the foreground. *(Ken Elks Collection)*

were inspected, and permission obtained for carrying passengers between Shepherdswell and Wingham Colliery halt. Despite publicity which suggested that the Richborough branch was almost ready for service, "only a furlong away from being completed" the reality was that only the contractor's line existed and approval for passengers on that part of the line was not obtained until 1924.

On 16 October 1916 passenger services were commenced from Shepherdswell to Wingham. The service and facilities were similar to Stephens' other railways, being very basic. Where no run round loop was provided the engine would have changed ends on its carriage by uncoupling before the station, running into a siding, and allowing the coach to roll into the platform under gravity. This rather dubious practice would not be condoned under today's modern safety standards.

The borings at Betteshanger were started in 1919, and subsequently sizeable coal seems were discovered. The Railway's Directors consulted Stephens and their surveyors over the possibilities of connecting with the new colliery. Plans were partly approved, but the new colliery already had a direct connection to the main line between Deal and Sandwich. Being the most recent of the Kent collieries, Betteshanger managed to out live the rest of the Kent coalfield.

In 1920 the line was continued for another half mile to Wingham Town station. The applications for additional extensions, made in 1914, were finally granted in 1920. These plans would have linked the railway to Snowdown, Canterbury and Deal, as well as several other minor collieries. The plans for a line to a new deep-water port between Birchington and Reculver were also applied for in 1914, but never renewed.

The development potential of the East Kent coalfield was demonstrated by the post war concept of "transforming the Garden of England into one vast coalfield" - as stated by the *Dover Express* of July 1921. This would have involved the opening of 18 extra collieries, with 70,000 additional workers and a consequent doubling of the population in East Kent. These alarming forecasts were made by Professor Abercrombie, in his regional survey for the development of East Kent. His projections now seem far removed from the reality, but if his plans had come into being then the area would have undoubtedly become radically different.

In 1921 Guilford Colliery finally surrendered to the problem of flooding and closed. Despite promising prospects it was to close without ever having raised any significant quantity of coal. The large engine house is still in place although in a derelict condition, previously having been in agricultural use. The latest plans are to convert it into dwellings. The branch to Guilford Colliery was officially abandoned in 1927, but was not however lifted until 1937.

The East Kent coalfield displayed signs of militancy comparable to the rest of national industry between the wars. In 1921 there were clashes between pickets, blacklegs, and Police at Snowdown Colliery. One third of East Kent miners were unemployed during the lockouts at Tilmanstone and Chislet Collieries in 1924. By the end of the General Strike in 1926 the mines' owners had locked out their work force. The 1926 strike was

Above: A view of the station at Shepherdswell, with the connection to the mainline railway branching off to the right and the platform and ticket office on the left. The building in the distance, beyond the end of the line, is the the South Eastern and Chatham Railway's goodshed. *(Lens of Sutton)*

followed by a general depression in British industry, which undoubtedly contributed to the failure of the Abercrombie plan.

The striking miners and their families survived mainly from private charity, which was surprisingly forthcoming from the often hostile locals. There was little strike pay and the Government's help was inconsequential. The events were fortunate to coincide with the fruit and hop-picking seasons. Once this seasonal work ran out the men slowly came back to work in the mines. Tilmanstone Colliery had some of the most modern and efficient equipment available, but this was of little use throughout the periods of strike. Tilmanstone Colliery was close to bankruptcy in 1924 and the strike did nothing to ease this situation.

Despite the below average working conditions and the high accident rate, the pay was very reasonable by national standards. After the 1926 strike and the opening of Betteshanger Colliery in the following year, greater numbers moved from other coalfields to find work in the area. Management at Tilmanstone Colliery endeavoured to advertise for 2,000 men in Northern and Midland newspapers. By 1930 the labour force had doubled to reach 5,000, and there was now a surplus of prospective miners, who were turned away. Many others returned home as a result of the poor working conditions

Above: Kent and East Sussex locomotive, Hecate, in use at Tilmanstone Colliery. The man in the sailor's uniform seems somewhat out of place! The locomotive probably saw more work there than it did on the KESR. *(Ken Elks Collection)*

Above: Eastry South halt, demonstrating the rural nature of the location. *(Author's Collection)*

According to the Secretary of the Kent branch of the National Union of Mineworkers in 1971 "A lot of men who came were militants from 1921 and 1926, men who were prepared to stand up and be counted. They were black-booked in the collieries and couldn't get jobs, so they came to Kent with assumed names." Many of the men who travelled to East Kent were known to have walked from Wales and the Midlands, whilst others sold all of their possessions to raise the train fare to their new lives. The mining community's roots are apparent by the multitude of dialects still present.

New stations were built in 1925 at Eastry South, and at Woodnesborough (Roman Road). The new colliery village at Elvington had the former Tilmanstone Colliery station replaced and renamed after it. Passenger services ran between Shepherdswell and Wingham three times daily, with an extra evening service on Saturdays. Along with this there was one train that ran only as far as Eastry, although two ran on Saturdays. The three weekday workings to Eythorne actually went on to Tilmanstone Colliery yard, with only one of these trips time tabled for a Saturday.

By 1925 the railway had managed to pay some interest to the Company's debenture holders, but was not in a position to issue a dividend to the shareholders. The original promises of untold fortunes now seemed very distant from the reality of the pitiable finances. In 1925 the Company made expenditures totalling £720,000, mainly relating to land purchases for extension schemes, but also including £300,000 for the underlying mineral rights. In 1926 the Southern Railway agreed to purchase all the remaining debentures and ordinary shares, at a cost of £300,000.

Despite aspirations to continue to Canterbury, the line only managed to extend by 770 yards, when, in 1925, the track was continued to Wingham Canterbury Road station. Work did begin on a cutting beyond the station, with a short length of track being laid in it. The station was equipped with a siding on the opposite side of the road and became the permanent terminus for the branch until closure, giving the main line a total length of 11¼ miles. It was originally named "Wingham", but later gained the more honest title of "Wingham Canterbury Road".

The Sandwich branch was finally opened for passenger traffic on 13 April 1925, with just one scheduled train a week, Saturdays only, leaving Shepherdswell at 3.10 pm and arriving back at 4.34 pm. It was not destined to be a success, as all passenger services on this section were terminated only three years after opening. Once passenger services ceased the line only saw occasional use, with infrequent loads of sugar beet, intermittent batches of Norwegian pit props or the odd wagon of blue Stonar clay being delivered via the port.

Richard Tilden Smith, the new owner of Tilmanstone Colliery objected to the high charges made for the movement of coal by both the EKR and the SR. In an attempt to reduce the cost of transport he had an aerial ropeway constructed in 1927, linking Tilmanstone Colliery and Dover Harbour. This reduced the railway's monopoly over the movement of Tilmanstone coal, but had no significant effect on the quantity of freight transported. The ropeway proved to be an ineffective means of moving coal, and closed long before the Second World War. Stephens' objected to the construction of the ropeway, and was keen to present a case for Richborough Port already being suited for transhipment of coal, or at least more so than Dover.

In 1927 the volume of freight traffic had shown a clear increase from the previous year, when it went from 107,197 tons to 222,230 tons, but by 1929 the number of men using the line to get to the collieries had reduced sufficiently for the miner's trains to cease. From 1931 until closure in 1948 there were only two passenger trains daily, one in the morning and the other in the evening, both running the complete length of the line. The Eastry - Richborough section closed for passenger trains on 31 October 1928, making it very doubtful whether any of the stations on this section ever produced any financial return. Stephens attempted to attract passengers by using the slogans, "Support The Local Line" and "Travel in safety, across country, away from crowded roads over home-made steel instead of imported rubber!" It is difficult to know which crowded roads in East Kent he was referring to!

The railway reached Richborough in 1928, but as a result of an argument with Pearson, Dorman Long trains did not run until the following year. By now the port was significantly less active in comparison to the World War I scene. The aspirations of the railway were to export coal from here, the principle reason for construction of the 2¼ mile long Sandwich branch. This was briefly achieved in 1929, when a small quantity of Snowdown coal was transferred. The use that this section of the line received could never have justified its construction. As a result of the poorly engineered bridges over the River Stour and main line railway, passenger trains were not allowed to reach the newly built station at the port.

The railway was in an agreement with St. Augustine Links Ltd, which stipulated that they would be provided with a port. However the agreement restricted the railway from building its own wharf. The railway entered a temporary agreement with Lord Greville, which allowed them use of Pearson's old tramway until St. Augustine's built their port. This agreement could never have been exercised as by 1918, and before the line reached Richborough, a new wharf had been built on the River Stour.

The conflict between the railway and the port's owners, Pearson, Dorman Long, were as a result of Lord Greville's land being taken over by the War Department. The railway made payments directly to the War Department, who later sold the port to Pearson, Dorman Long. As a result long disputes erupted over access to Pearson's wharf. The failure of Richborough in exporting coal is intriguing, given Pearson, Dorman Long's association with the Kent coalfield. This rather suggests that Pearson, Dorman Long were trying to avoid dealing with the East Kent Light Railway. Relationships were undoubtedly not helped by the line's clumsy image.

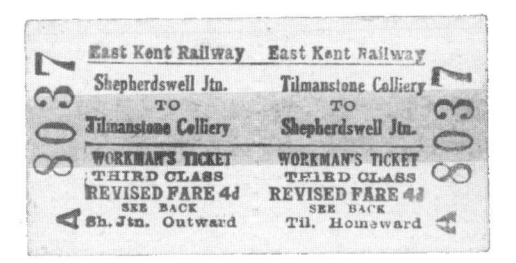

Left: A work man's ticket. *(Author's collection)*

Below: Locomotive No. 2, Walton Park, outside the engine shed at Shepherdswell. *(Lens of Sutton)*

The Railway Magazine of March 1937 reported that:

"The Company planned to develop Richborough as a coal port using lines and wharves laid down by Messrs Pearson's in connection with the Dover Harbour Admiralty Works. The train ferry births and other works were constructed by the Government for War service, but despite the association of Messrs Pearson, Dorman Long with the coal field and port since, the Railway Company has not succeeded in getting any large quantity of coal routed via the port, mainly owing to the changed circumstances of the British coal export trade, a misfortune which could not have been foreseen in 1911."

This emphasised the failure of the Richborough branch, as by the time that it was completed it had little purpose.

An application was made in 1927 to have the Canterbury and Deal extensions diverted. Stephens was the main force behind the lines continual expansion, and after his death on 23 October 1931 all extension projects seem to have been abandoned. The Deal extension was nearing completion as most of the track bed had been levelled and some ballast laid in preparation for the track. Earth works on the Canterbury extension scheme had progressed as far as Stodmarsh Junction, whilst the Birchington line was awaiting a Light Railway Order. The line continued to be administered from Stephens' Tonbridge office, at 23 Salford Terrace. Stephens never received any sizeable reward for his work on the line. In 1923 he was however given a large number of low value shares. He later had to surrender his shares, together with his Directorship to give way to representatives from the Southern Railway.

It took the lines Directors until 1932 to appoint Mr William H. Austen as General Manager, later appointed as Official Receiver. He had been Stephens' assistant for some time and was not only now in charge of the East Kent Railway, but also a number of Stephens' other lines. The mainstay of the line was as ever the freight traffic. During 1935 the railway carried 240,796 tons of coal, 7,048 ton of general freight, 2,118 tons of other minerals and 336 head of livestock. This shows a healthy increase on the 1918 figures, with the quantity of coal having nearly doubled.

Austen recommended that the Port Richborough line be closed in 1937, as it was now losing some £60 per annum, despite having been closed for passenger trains nearly ten years. It was however retained, although maintenance ceased eventually rendering the primitive viaduct unsafe. The passenger figures would appear to have been damaged by the reduction in the number of men travelling over the system to work at the mines, most of them either walked, cycled or went by bus.

The running of the railway was again interrupted by hostilities, in the shape of World War II. On the 1 September 1939 the line was brought under the control of the Minister of War Transport, with Port Richborough being used to despatch supplies to the British Expeditionary Forces in France. Staple station also played its part in the action, with large ammunition stores being based at the nearby RAF station. So that the railway could cope with the extra traffic generated by the RAF they created an office at Staple by grounding the body of the ex-Cheshire Lines Committee carriage (EKR No. 3). The station was later requisitioned from 18 May until July, whilst a dummy aerodrome was constructed at Ash.

The Railway Executive Committee realised the potential value of the EKR during the war, as concerns over the Kent coast line from Dover to Ramsgate being made impassable led them to maintain the branch as a back up measure. In September 1940 the line again found itself helping the War effort by housing the large calibre rail-mounted guns of the 2nd Super Heavy Regiment, Royal Artillery. Two 12 inch guns of 8th Battery were stationed at Eythorne, together with a section of 5th Battery with another 12 inch gun. The guns were stored in the siding formed by the remnant of the Guilford Colliery branch, behind Eythorne Court, which was used as the battery's headquarters. The battery moved to Elham in 1942.

Hammill brick works halted production during the war years as their buildings were used for the storage of food supplies that were delivered by way of the railway to the work's siding. It was necessary to upgrade some of the track when the railway became home to the 12 inch Howitzer and 9.2 inch mobile railway guns, together with War Department locomotives. The wartime activities on the line caused their fair share of damage, and compensation was eventually set at £600 per annum.

After the War ended in 1945 the line returned back to its casual existence. The management decided to attempt to smarten the railway up. Repairs were made to buildings and rolling stock, with a number of the older vehicles being scrapped. Some new coaching stock was purchased, with a corporate green livery being adopted. The number of trains remained at two per day, whilst the majority of traffic was still being generated by Tilmanstone

Above: Locomotive No. 1 at Shepherdswell, complete with the rebuilt cab. *(Lens of Sutton)*

Colliery. Like the number of passengers, the transport of local freight carried saw significant decline. The future of the line and the Kent coal industry would soon be dramatically altered by the post-World War II wave of nationalisation. Professor Abercrombie's 1921 dream of industrialising Kent was now well and truly lost. Much to the delight of the natives Kent was destined to remain as the picturesque "Garden of England".

The four remaining Kent Collieries, Betteshanger, Tilmanstone, Chislet and Snowdown, were nationalised under the control of the National Coal Board in January 1947. The East Kent Railway was to keep its independence slightly longer, being nationalised under British Railways on 8 May 1948. With only 556 passengers using the system in 1947 services were rendered uneconomical. All passenger traffic was withdrawn on the 1 November 1948. The line from Eastry to Richborough was finally closed on 27 October 1949, its fate having been delayed some 12 years since Austen's recommendations.

Track lifting began on 1 January 1950, starting with the line from Eastry to Richborough. The branch west of Eastry was next to go being closed on 25 July 1950, with the line north of Eythorne being closed on 1 March 1951. The railway was destined to become nothing more than a mineral line, relying on Tilmanstone Colliery to generate its traffic. The line noticeably became part of the national system on 1 July 1951, when all the lines remaining locomotives were withdrawn and replaced with engines working from Dover.

Above: British Railway's diesel electric locomotive, No. 4110 (now 09022) is seen hauling a train of full coal wagons on 31 August 1972. *(Richard Stumpf)*

The miners strike in 1984 has been held responsible for the coal traffic quitting the line, although the industry's demise now seems inevitable. The whole fiasco of the East Kent Railway and indeed the East Kent coalfield was now moving near to extinction. Tilmanstone Colliery was closed in October 1985, with the rest of the industry in Kent meeting a similar fate. The site at Tilmanstone was flattened, unlike that of Snowdown where the derelict buildings create a haunting memory of the aspirations of the Kent coalfield. As the line now had no purpose it was officially closed on 31 December 1987.

The unique line was not however to be lost totally as in November 1985 the East Kent Light Railway Society was established to preserve the remaining section of track between Shepherdswell and Tilmanstone. Passenger services were again run when a diesel multiple unit reopened the line from Shepherdswell to Eythorne on 24 June 1995. The task of returning the line to a satisfactory standard for the use of passenger trains was very daunting, reflecting the years of neglect. The latest plans are to take the line back into the colliery site, by replacing the missing bridge. These proposals envisage the construction of a museum depicting the story of the Kent coalfield, which would serve as a fitting tribute to the now extinct local industry.

Above: A smart looking Class 107 diesel multiple unit, at Shepherdswell station, June 1996. Colonel Stephens would surely have approved of the operation of the line by preservationists with such motive power, having pioneered the use of railcars on some of his other railways. *(Author)*

THE STATIONS

Shepherdswell was provided with a station separate to that of the South Eastern and Chatham Railway. It was reached by a footpath from the main line station, being situated in a chalk cutting. A circular iron hut served as the original waiting room, with two garden shed type buildings of differing size half way down the platform, acting as a ticket office. A later building was constructed again resembling two sheds. This time they were of the same size and were connected by the roof that formed a canopy between them. This later building was likely to have been composed of parts of the earlier wooden huts, and was built in front of the iron shed. The iron hut was later used as a parcel's office with a wooden building perched on the bank behind the station, serving as the Company's office.

It was at Shepherdswell that the line's engine shed and workshop were located. The water for the locomotives came from a reservoir located on high ground North of the shed. In common with Stephens' other lines he deplored the idea of paying water rates, and endeavoured to find more economical solutions. The maintenance facilities were sparse, but did not deter the staff in performing the most involved of repairs and overhauls. Earth works were prepared for a new connection to the South Eastern and Chatham Railway, involving an embankment and cutting to the North of the station. The link was never completed; the track that was partly laid being used as a siding.

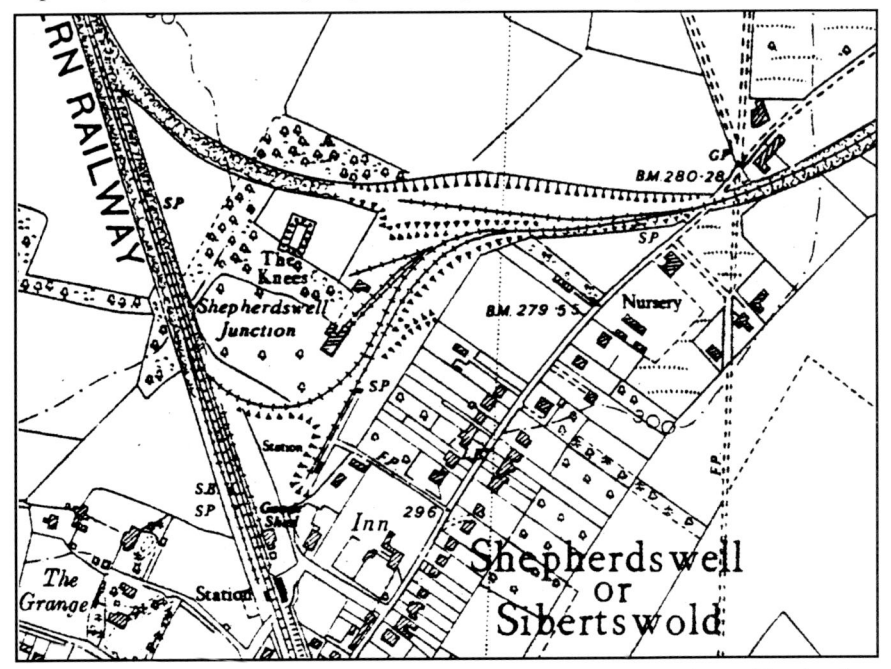

Above: An enlargement of the 6" 1937 revision of the 1906 map shows Shepherdswell station, with the intended spur to the mainline north of the site.

Above: A view of Eythorne station with the Tilmanstone Colliery head gear in the distance, 3 March 1951. The line continues straight on to Eastry, whilst the branch on the right connects to the Colliery. *(Pamlin Prints)*

Below: The earthworks for the Eythorne triangle can be clearly seen on this enlargement of the 1937 revision of the 1906 map, together with the station site.

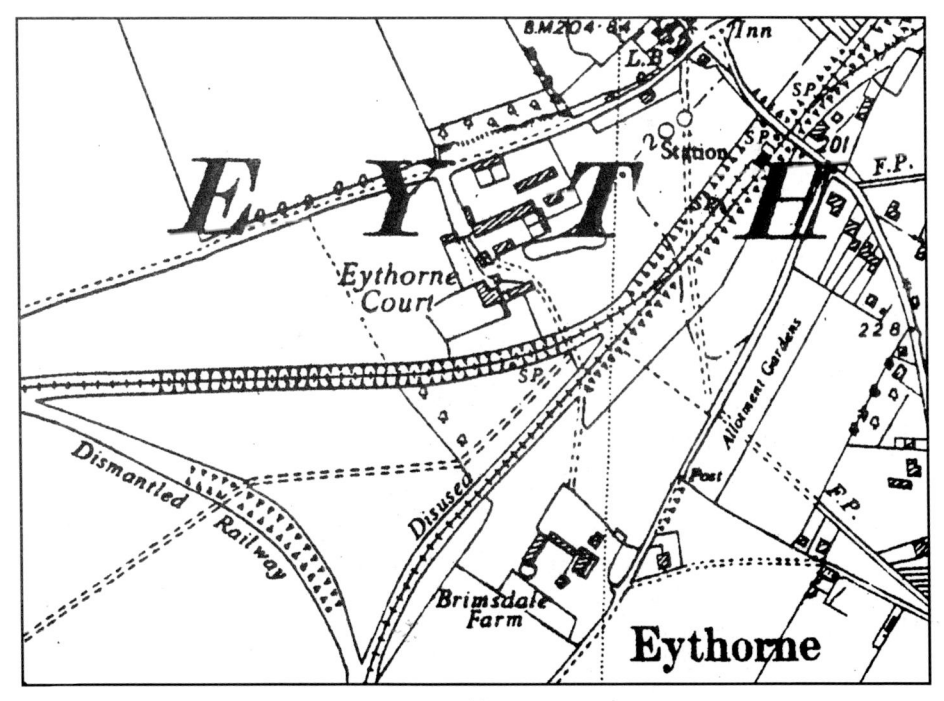

Eythorne served as the junction for the lines to Guilford Colliery and Tilmanstone Colliery. The station consisted of two wooden buildings on a platform built of sleepers with an ash in-fill. The early wooden buildings were replaced by a brick built structure, similar to that at Staple, which functioned as a ticket office, stores and waiting room. A brick built hut near the road initially housed a ground frame to control the signals. There was a passing loop and siding provided, with a second siding being added a later date. Had all the proposed lines been completed then the station would have become very busy as the lines main junction.

Elvington halt was originally opened as Tilmanstone Colliery Halt, but was renamed to serve the newly built mining community in 1925. The platform was originally timber faced but was rebuilt at the same time as being renamed, the new platform having a brick front. Miners' trains now ran directly to Tilmanstone, where a simple platform may have been provided. Knowlton Halt was of simple construction, having a wooden face to the platform, and originally being furnished with a wooden shelter. The station was little used, probably owing to it being located some distance from the village. Eastry South Halt was built in 1925, being well situated for a good part of the village. It had a wooden faced platform, of similar construction to that at Knowlton.

Eastry station became the junction for the lines to Wingham and Richborough. The station was equipped with a loop and siding, which were controlled by signals worked from a ground frame. It was able to boast a covered ground frame, consisting of a small wooden hut. The station building was of a similar style to the later building at Shepherdswell, consisting of two sheds with a common roof. The platform was brick built and later gained a grounded box van body at one end. The length of the platform was eventually reduced, probably in an attempt to diminish maintenance costs.

Left: A group of passengers waiting for their train at Wingham Town station. Their smiles suggest that they have yet to experience a ride in an East Kent Railway carriage! *(Lens of Sutton)*

LOCOMOTIVES

The first locomotive to work on the East Kent Railway arrived in 1911 initially belonging to the line's Contractor. It was built by Fox Walker and Co. in 1875 for the Whitland and Cardigan Railway. After the aforementioned line was absorbed by the Great Western Railway in 1886 the locomotive was renumbered in their series as No. 1386, and was subsequently rebuilt at Swindon in 1896. By 1911 the locomotive had been sold for use at Bute Docks, being resold for use on the EKR later in the same year. After ownership passed to the East Kent Railway it became No. 1. As originally built it was a half cab design, later receiving a wooden back extension to the cab before a permanent metal structure was added. It was regularly used on the system up to the 1930s, eventually being scrapped in 1938.

The second locomotive to work on the line was an 0-4-0 Barclay that presumably belonged to the Contractors. The *Kentish Gazette* of 5 July 1913 records there being two locomotives at work on the Company's property, being before the arrival of No. 2. This supports the photograph of a Barclay locomotive at Ash. Its stay on the line appears to have been quite short; it is likely that it left when the Contractors completed their work.

The *Kentish Gazette* report noted that there were two new locomotives under construction for the line. There is photographic evidence of an 0-6-0 locomotive built by Hawthorn Leslie in 1914, bearing the name *Gabrielle*, after Arthur Burr's granddaughter, and with "East Kent Railway" written across the side tank. It never arrived on the line, supposedly having been requisitioned for the War effort. It seems likely that the railway could not afford to complete the locomotive's purchase, given their financial difficulties. An almost identical locomotive was supplied to the Plymouth, Devonport & South Western Railway in 1907, where Stephens was also engineer.

Stephens' Kent and East Sussex Railway loaned a locomotive, in the shape of 0-8-0 *Hecate*. It was built for the KESR in 1904 by Hawthorn, Leslie. During its stay from 1916 to 1919 it was mainly used for shunting at Tilmanstone Colliery. Its large wheelbase was found to be unsuitable for the Colliery sidings, and it ceased to be used as more appropriate motive power arrived. It was intended for the steeply graded Maidstone section of the KESR, which was never built. It proved too big to be useful on the existing KESR and was sold to the Southern Railway in 1932 and numbered as 949.

In 1917 another locomotive appeared on the railway, in the shape of No. 2 *Walton Park*. It was built by Hudswell Clarke in 1908 for Stephen's Weston, Clevedon & Portishead Railway. It is reputed to have been sold to his Shropshire & Montgomeryshire Railway in 1913, from whence it was quickly transferred to the EKR. Walton Park was a station on the W. C. & P., the locomotive following Stephens' tradition of naming engines after his lines' stations. It was sold for scrap in 1943 to T. W. Ward, but was later found at Purfleet in working order. Before being scrapped in 1957 it was seen working at Hastings Gas Works.

In 1918 the railway purchased another engine, which followed on in the series as No. 3, in the shape of former London South Western No. 0394. The 0-6-0 tender engine was built by Beyer Peacock for William Adams in 1880, to Beattie's design. Following their success in North Devon this class of locomotive was known as the "Ilfracombe Goods". After 1900 this class of engine were placed on the duplicate list of surplus engines and either sold off or scrapped. Stephens acquired six of the locomotives for use on his lines. When the boiler was condemned it was left standing at Shepherdswell until being scrapped in 1934.

Locomotive No. 4 came to the line in 1919, being only 2 years old. It was built by Kerr, Stuart & Co. for the Inland Waterways Docks Department, for use at Richborough. Initially it was purchased by a group of Colliery owners who leased it to the railway. It was scrapped in 1949, having spent one year under the control of British Railways as No. 30948. The sturdy looking 0-6-0 tank locomotive was regarded as the lines best engine, probably due to its mere infancy in comparison with its ageing colleagues. It was normally employed on the heavy coal trains from Tilmanstone Colliery.

By 1919 the railway's motley collection of locomotives had grown by the addition of No. 5, an Adams Radial Tank, at a cost of £900 from the Disposals Commission. It was built in 1885 by Neilson and Co. for the London South Western Railway, under whom it was numbered as 488. After being commandeered by the Ministry of Supplies in 1917, it was later resold to the EKR. The Southern Railway purchased the locomotive in 1948 as they found this ageing design ideal for their Lyme Regis branch line. Despite a purchase price of £120 it had to undergo an extensive overhaul at Eastleigh costing over £1600. It is now resident on the Bluebell Railway, where it was preserved following withdrawal in 1961.

Above: Locomotive No. 4, the pride of the Railway's fleet. *(Ken Elks Collection)*

Above: The Adams Radial Tank, locomotive No. 5. This is the only surviving engine from the line's varied collection. *(Lens of Sutton)*

Besides the resident locomotives the line often played host to other engines. Kent and East Sussex Railway No. 2, *Northiam* was loaned to the Railway, although there seems to be considerable contradiction as to the time and length of its visits. It is thought to have been first loan to the EKR in 1912 until some time after 1914, but there is no evidence to support this. It's visit from circa 1921 until 1929 has more substance behind it, having been both photographed and noted in the *Railway Magazine*. It was built for the KESR in 1900 by Hawthorn Leslie. The locomotive was destined for fame when it played the part of *Gladstone* in the film *Oh! Mr Porter*.

In May 1923 the Railway purchased SECR No. 372, which became EKR No. 6. It was built in 1891 by Sharp Stewart to Stirling's O class design. In 1931 it travelled to Ashford to receive a domed boiler and was reclassified as an O1, this made it an interesting hybrid as the other O1s received other additional modifications when rebuilt. Under nationalisation it became No. 31372, but was scrapped before being renumbered. This type of locomotive enjoyed a successful career on the line, implied by the subsequent purchase of similar engines. No. 6 in particular proved to be the mainstay of the line's locomotives.

Locomotive No. 7 was purchased in 1925 at a cost of £360. It originated from the London South Western Railway, where it was numbered 0127. It was constructed in 1882 to Beattie's design by Beyer Peacock. It was obtained from the War Office who commandeered it in 1917. It was finally scrapped in 1946 when the boiler became life expired.

Another ex SER O class was purchased in 1928 by the Railway, owing to the poor condition of the railway's other engines. It was built in 1891, and was numbered (A)376 under the Southern Railway, becoming No. 8 in the EKR's fleet. It was found to be in a bad condition upon arrival, and the Company did what repairs they could afford. Maintenance proved to be too costly for the locomotive, and it was subsequently sold for scrap in 1934 together with No. 3.

The line's next purchase was an O1 class in 1935, presumably as a replacement for the disappointing No. 8. It had the same origin as Nos. 6 & 8 having been built in 1891 by Sharp, Stewart & Co. It was rebuilt in 1908 to O1 standards when it received the angular Wainwright cab, as oppose to the original Stirling cabs of Nos. 6 and 8. Under the Southern Railway it was numbered as (A)383. It was overhauled at Ashford prior to arrival on the line and was numbered out of series as EKR No. 100. The Ashford painters had not been told what number to apply and assumed that this would not conflict with the lines other engines. From 1946 it became No. 2, after *Walton Park* was scrapped. It was passed over to British Railways upon nationalisation of the EKR, and survived until 1955 as No. 31383.

The railway purchased its last locomotive in the shape of another Southern Railway O1 class. Being of the same origin as No. 100, it was rebuilt to O1 standards in 1909. It was purchased in September 1944, and retained its Southern Railway livery and number, merely being given an "EKR" prefix (EKR No. 1371). It survived until nationalisation, but was scrapped in 1949 before being renumbered as BR No. 31371. To help with traffic over the Tilmanstone branch the Southern Railway lent the line one of its O1 class, No. 1379, briefly during World War II.

Above: No. 6 hauls its lone carriage out of the platform at Shepherdswell station, 25 September 1948. *(James Aston)*

British Railways' Stirling O1s provided the line with its motive power after nationalisation. They were tried and tested in the shape of the EKR owned class members, and proved to be ideal for the line. The coal trains remained steam hauled for a further decade after nationalisation. The most suitable replacements for the O1s were the newly built class 08 and 09 diesel shunters. Much of the line's light railway charm had by now been lost, aided by the bland character of the modern diesel engines. The predictable operation was only occasionally broken, often by one of the visiting rail tours. Before the line closed the class 73 electro-diesel saw some use on the line, being employed on coal trains.

Left: This dog ticket is not as much of a bargain as it seems, given that the system was never more than 18 miles long! (Ken Elks Collection)

Below: East Kent Railway No. 1371 at Shepherdswell, 25 September 1948. This locomotive was the last in the succession of second hand engines purchased for use on the line. (James Aston)

CARRIAGES

Little is known about the early history of the line's coaching stock. Information is more forthcoming after 1920, but compiling a definitive list involves an element of assumption. There appear to be few photographs of some carriages, and often the paintwork is in such a poor state that their number cannot be identified.

At the time of opening the Company only owned one coach, which was a vestibule bogie brake previously employed by the KESR. A North London Railway four-wheeled passenger brake is thought to have arrived some time after 1912, probably also having come from the KESR. In 1919 the line purchased a Cheshire Lines Committee four wheeled 3rd. Three London Chatham and Dover Railway four wheelers were acquired in 1920. Later purchases involved the acquisition of a London South Western six-wheeled carriage and two London Chatham and Dover Railway six wheeled carriages. Two London South Western corridor bogie coaches were brought in 1946, bringing with them a new standard of comfort to the line. A South Eastern and Chatham Railway brake van was acquired in the latter days of the line's life. The standard livery was brown or grey, until 1945 when all remaining stock was painted dark green.

GOODS STOCK

It is difficult to compose a finite list as stock was often broken up, with the vacant numbers in the series being filled with new stock. The list in Appendix II is representative of the line's goods stock circa 1930, save the last three items. The standard livery was either black or brown, with the letters E.K.R. or East Kent Railway, and the wagon's number being applied in white. There are early photographs showing Tilmanstone Colliery wagons, but coal traffic was normally carried in wagons from one of the main line companies. In the latter years of the line's life coal was transported in steel mineral wagons or hopper wagons.

Above: The Railway's hand crane. *(Lens of Sutton)*

Above: Two ex. LCDR carriages in the station at Shepherdswell. *(Lens of Suton)*

Below: British Railway's No. 31425 at the throat of Tilmanstone Colliery yard, 8 July 1959. *(James Aston)*

APPENDIX I - Locomotives

No.	Class	Config.	Maker	Works	Built	Acquired	Withdrawn (Scrapped)
1	-	0-6-0ST	FW	271	1875	1911	1934 (1936)
2	-	0-6-0ST	HC	823	1908	1916	1941 (1959)
3	315	0-6-0	BP	2042	1880	1916	1928 (1934)
4	-	0-6-0T	KS	3067	1917	1919	1949
5	415	4-4-2T	NC	3209	1882	1919	1939*
6	O	0-6-0	SS	3714	1891	1923	1949
7	330	0-6-0ST	BP	2125	1882	1924	1941 (1946)
8	O	0-6-0	SS	3718	1893	1928	1934
100 (2)	O1	0-6-0	SS	3950	1893	1935	1955
1317	O1	0-6-0	SS	3713	1891	1944	1949

* No. 5 is now preserved on the Bluebell Line, Sussex.

FW	Fox, Walker & Co.
HC	Hudswell, Clarke
BP	Beyer, Peacock
KS	Kerr, Stuart
NC	Neilson & Co.
SS	Sharp, Stewart

APPENDIX II - Wagons

No.	Description
1	Ex LBSCR 12 ton breakdown crane. Scrapped *c.* 1948.
2	Ex LMS low sided wagon.
3	Four wheeled truck for crane.
4-34	Wagons, mainly for carrying coal.
35	Low sided drop wagon.
36	High sided coal wagons.
37	High sided coal wagons.
38	Bolster wagon used as match truck for crane.
39	Open wagons.
58	Ex SECR brake van.
59	Ex LSWR 10 ton brake van.
60	Ex LSWR 10 ton brake van.

APPENDIX III - Carriages

No.	Type	Origin	Acquired	Scrapped
1	41' Bogie Saloon Brake Composite	KESR	1912	1948
2	4 wheeled Full Brake	NLR/KESR		1948
3	4 wheeled 5 Compartment 3rd	CLC/KESR	1919	1940*
4	6 wheeled 4 Compartment 1st & 2nd Brake Composite	MR		1948
5	6 wheeled 3 Compartment 3rd Brake	LSWR		1948
6	4 wheeled 4 Compartment 1st	GER/KESR		1937
7	4 wheeled 4 Compartment 1st	LCDR	1920	1948
8	4 wheeled 4 Compartment 3rd	LCDR	1920	1948
9	4 wheeled 3 Compartment 3rd Brake	LCDR	1920	1948
10	6 wheeled 3 Compartment 3rd & 1st Brake Composite	LCDR	1926	1946
11	6 wheeled 3 Compartment 3rd Brake Composite	LCDR	1926	1946
5*	Bogie Corridor 5 Compartment 2nd Brake	LSWR	1946	1948
6*	Bogie Corridor 5 Compartment 2nd Brake	LSWR	1946	1948

* No. 3 was grounded and used as an office at Staple during World War II.
* Nos. 5 & 6 were reissued in 1946.

KESR   Kent and East Sussex Railway
NLR   North London Railway
CLC   Cheshire Lines Committee
MR   Midland Railway
GER   Great Eastern Railway
LCDR   London, Chatham and Dover Railway
LSWR   London and South Western Railway

Above: An extract from the Southern Railway's 1937 summer timetable.

APPENDIX IV - Extensions

1	Shepherdswell to Richborough	1911
2	Wingham to Eastry	1911
3.	Conection between railways Nos. 1 and 2 at Eastry	Not authorised
4	Guilford Colliery branch from Eythorne	1911
5	Eythorne to Betteshanger via Tilmanstone Colliery	1911
6	Wingham to Goodnestone	Not authorised
7	Spur from No. 6 at Wingham to form a triangular junction	Not authorised
8	Spur from Guilford branch to Eythorne	1911
9	Richborough Castle siding	1911
10	Incompleted northern spur with SECR at Shepherdswell	1911
11	Eythorne to Mongeham	1911
12	Guilford to Maydensole	1911
13	Guilford to SECR at Stonehall	1911
14	Woodnesborough Colliery branch from No. 2	1911
15	Wickhambreux Colliery branch from Wingham	1912
16	Ripple Colliery branch from Mongeham	1912
17	Connection from Mongeham to Poison Cross	Not authorised
18	Woodnesborough to Snowdown	1920
19	Mongeham to Deal	1920
20	Junction from No. 19 to SECR at Deal	1920
21	Not mentioned in 1914 application	Not authorised
22	Wickhambreux to SECR at Canterbury	1920
23	Guilford to Drellingore	1920
24	Stonehall to Drellingore	1920
25	Not mentioned in 1914 application	Not authorised
26	Northbourne branch from No. 11	1920
27	Spur to Wingham Colliery from No. 2	1920
28	Junction from No. 1 to tramway at Richborough Old Wharf	1920
29	Wickhambreux to Birchington	Not authorised
30	Junction from No. 29 to SECR at Sarre	Not authorised
31	Spur from No. 29 to SECR near Birchington	Not authorised
32	Spur from No. 29 to SECR near Birchington	Not authorised
33	Wingham to Wickhambreux cut-off line	1931
34	Junction from No. 1 to SECR near Sandwich	Not authorised
35	Spur from No. 34 to SECR	Not authorised
36	Junction from No. 15 to SECR near Chislet	Not authorised
37	Improved version of railway No. 11	1931
38	Tilmanstone Colliery to main line north of Elvington	Not authorised
39	Junction from No. 36 to SECR near Chislet	Not authorised
40	Extension of Richborough Castle siding	Not authorised

"Not authorised" also includes the company withdrawing an application before approval.

EAST KENT RAILWAY.

NOTICE.

Special Workmen's Trains will run as under every Weekday :—

DOWN TRAINS		N.S.	S.O.
	a.m.	p.m.	p.m.
Shepherdswell .... dep.	5 13	9 30	7 20
Eythorne .... ,,	5 20	9 37	7 27
Tilmanstone Colliery .... ,,	5 23	9 40	7 30
Tilmanstone Village & Knowlton ,,	5 27	Stop.	7 34
Eastry .... arr.	5 34		7 41

UP TRAINS		N.S.	S.O.
	a.m.	p.m.	p.m.
Eastry .... dep.	5 42	—	7 50
Tilmanstone Village & Knowlton ,,	5 49	—	7 57
Tilmanstone Colliery ... { arrive	5 53	—	8 1
{ dept.	6 20	10 20	
Eythorne .... ,,	6 24	10 24	8 6
Shepherdswell .... ,,	6 30	10 30	8 12

N.S.—Not Saturdays.   S.O.—Saturdays only.

FARES :—
3rd Class.

Shepherdswell to Eastry or Tilmanstone Colliery - -	2d.
Shepherdswell to Eastry or Tilmanstone Colliery & return	3d.
Tilmanstone Colliery to Shepherdswell - - -	2d.
Tilmanstone Colliery to Eastry & return - - -	4d.
Eastry to Tilmanstone Colliery & return - - -	4d.

These Fares are only available for Workmen travelling by above Special Trains. Ordinary Fares will be charged by ordinary Trains.

Tonbridge,
October, 1916.

H. F. STEPHENS,
General Manager.

"Support the Local Line."
EAST KENT RAILWAY.
TIME TABLE.
OCTOBER 16th, 1916,
AND UNTIL FURTHER NOTICE.

DOWN TRAINS. **WEEK DAYS.**

MILES.		a.m.	a.m.	p.m.	p.m.
	London, Victoria......dep.	5 50	10 45	2ns15	1so34
S.E. & C.R.	Canterbury East .... ,,	8 10	12 32	4ns31	3so51
	Dover Priory .... ,,	9 35	1 10	4 45	
	Deal .... ,,	8b42	11 15	3 5	
—	Shepherdswell Jn., E.K.Rly.dep.	10 10	1 32	5 10	
1¾	Eythorne .... ,,	10 17	1 38	5 17	
2½	Tilmanstone Colliery .... ,,	10 20	1 41	5 20	
—	Tilmanstone Village & Knowlton,,	10 24	1 45	5 24	
5¾	Eastry, for Sandwich .... ,,	10 31	1 52	5 31	
6½	Woodnesborough & Hammill ,,	10 35	1 56	5 35	
8	Ash Town..................... ,,	10 40	2 1	5 40	
8¾	Staple .... ,,	10 44	2 5	5 44	
10¼	Wingham .... arr.	10 50	2 11	5 56	

UP TRAINS. **WEEK DAYS.**

MILES.		a.m.	p.m.	p.m.	p.m.
—	Wingham..................dep.	10 55	2 14	6 0	
1½	Staple .... ,,	11 7	2 25	s	
2¼	Ash Town..................... ,,	11 11	2 29	6 13	
3¾	Woodnesborough & Hammill ,,	11 15	2 33	6 16	
4½	Eastry, for Sandwich .... ,,	11 20	2 38	6 21	
—	Tilmanstone Village & Knowlton,,	s	s	s	
7¾	Tilmanstone Colliery .... ,,	11 30	2 48	6 31	
8½	Eythorne .... ,,	11 35	2 53	6 36	
10¼	Shepherdswell Jn., E.K.Rly.arr.	11 41	2 58	6 42	
	Deal .... ,,	—	b5s42	7 17	
S.E. & C.R.	Dover Priory .... ,,	1 14	3 17	7 3	
	Canterbury East .... ,,	12 25	3 49	6 29	
	London, Victoria......... ,,	2 47	6 12	8 37	

b—via Dover Priory. n.s.—Not Saturdays. s—Stops by signal to pick up or set down passengers s.o.—Saturdays only.
°—On Saturdays arrives 5-2 p.m.

Special arrangements for quick and cheap delivery of parcels and goods.   Special trips arranged as required.

Every effort will be made to connect with the trains of S. E. & C. Rly. as shewn, but the same will not be guaranteed.

TONBRIDGE,   H. F. STEPHENS,
  October, 1916.   *General Manager.*